MW00737725

For
Nadine

May your life
always know love
because you have
a soul purpose

Best
wishes

[signature]

To
Nadine
Very ... I ...
... you I ...

HOW WOULD YOU LIKE YOUR WORLD TODAY?

A COLLECTION OF CONTEMPORARY LOVE POETRY

BY

HERMENE HARTMAN

CREDITS

PUBLISHER

HARTMAN PUBLISHING GROUP
19 North Sangamon
Chicago, Illinois 60607-2613
312/822..0202
www.ndigo.com

GRAPHIC DESIGNER
CREATIVE CONSULTANT

JEFFERY A. REED

www.joyeuxdesigns.com

Copyright © by 2010 Hermene Hartman

ISBN Number   10   0983357404

ISBN Number   13   978-09 8335740-7

For those who have been barefoot in love,
danced with love
and who know love.

die liebe

amour

愛

SZERETET

애정

kaerlighed

kärlek

喜爱

SAYANG

láska

IRMASTUS

LOVE

amore

These poems are for women who have married, divorced and found comfort in being single. They have been my kept writings, not to be shared. My cousin, Linda, has read many of these poems and always encouraged a book. My friend Melody did the same. They both have known different sides of these poems.

And then he came and I wanted to share them. I started writing poems for Reggie and I didn't know why. I realized he sparked a love that desired to communicate. I wanted to share this poetry. Time to love again, to care enough to want to write a poem and leave it on the pillow.

And then he came
I wasn't looking for him but I was waiting
He came with a wonderful blend of life
And assured with a clear certainty
I wanted him to know me, from the beauty of my inner being
From haute couture to jeans
Laughing
The gourmet of my essence
And the spirit of dancing
With a lovely emotional honesty.

die liebe

amour

愛

SZERETET

amigurumi

IRMASTUS

kaerlighed

애정

SAYANG

kärlek

喜爱

láska

LOVE

amore

PREFACE

LOVE is a mighty splendid thing.
It graces when least expected; it overwhelms without consent.

And it haunts when it fades.

LOVE is a mixed bag of interpretations, expectations and obligations.

It desires maintenance; it requires authenticity.

And it won't be ignored.

Volumes have been written about LOVE, and more will be written without exhaust

How Would You Like Your World Today? speaks to love's highs, lows and in-betweens–as seen through a real woman's eyes.

This collection of poetry speaks to the LOVE that builds you up; and the love that wears you down.

It speaks to the LOVE that makes you behave other than yourself; and the LOVE that makes you discover who you really are.

From flirtation to maturation to emancipation,
How Would You Like Your World Today? speaks the language of love.

And it speaks to us all.

—Zondra Hughes

die liebe

amour

SZERETET

ARMASTUS

애정

kaerlighed

kärlek

SAYANG

喜爱

láska

LOVE

amore

TABLE OF CONTENTS

Photo Courtesy of ERNEST COLLINS PHOTOGRAPHY

didn't know I could write poetry.

I was married for a decade. My husband went away on a business trip and after a mere three days, I missed him dearly.

I wanted him to know he was missed.

I wrote my fleeting thoughts as I listened to my favorite jazz. Between sips of wine these poems were written in contemplation with reflection.

I left the poem on his pillow.

Soon, every time my husband went away, he came home to poems on his pillow. I am basically shy, and I haven't shared my poetry with many, only a few precious friends at special times, and always as a gift.

When we parted, I cherished this nice collection of poems. They have been tucked away. I continued to write poetry in my very private moments. These poems have been written over a period of years, sparked by my heart's journey from rapture to capture, from fleeting flirtations to relationships abundant in sensual sensibility.

These words represent the intimate evolution of friendships from first hellos to final departures.

Love is a gift and words are proof of love's authenticity.

My uncle, the renowned jazz singer Johnny Hartman, had a keen ear and a beautiful voice; to him, there was nothing better than a great ballad with lovely lyrics—he loved a great love song.

As a child, my uncle taught me to recognize the meaning of lyrics. Johnny Hartman was a master of the lyric; "listen to the words" he would say. He taught me the song's romantic sensibility. His philosophy was that lyrics should tell a story; a singer was the interpreter. He was an incurable romantic.

My uncle taught me to listen to lyric. We made a game of it; and we played while riding in the car, walking, looking at TV and even at dinner.

As he traveled the world, he would call on Sunday mornings. When he came home, we listened to the great jazz singers, Dinah Washington, Sarah Vaughan, Arthur Prysock, Frank Sinatra, Nat King Cole, Lena Horne, and Billy Eckstine among them. He also loved Billy Strayhorn, Cole Porter and George Gershwin. These were music lessons.

Of course, I didn't fully understand any of it until I was well grown. The last song we engaged was the popular disco tune, "I Will Survive."

"Listen to the lyrics," he told me. My uncle thought it was a great love song and he performed it with an entirely different spin—he sung it as a ballad. The lyric and the reinterpretation were exquisite; it was a different song with an aching meaning.

From those musical dialogues, I learned and began to write word compositions that became my poetry, that search music.

This is a book of **LOVE**.

Over the years I have written about manships—expressions, thoughts, and sentiments, about men who have stirred my heart and awakened my muse.

The title poem, *How Would You Like Your World Today?*, was written for my father and uncle; at the time, I was searching for Christmas gifts for them and a tie just didn't work. I wondered, if I could give them a world, what would be in it? What wonderful experience might bear repeating?

These poems represent the sense of a passionate woman. They represent a gypsy woman, a professional, a grown child, a woman-being and becoming one who thought she might not know real love again.

These poems represent the prosperity of love with a rendezvous of romance. Some of these feelings are new and divine. I thought this romantic mindset would never be revealed again. But these feelings have resurfaced—this time with a deeper, magical spark.

These poems are for women who know marriage, divorce and have found comfort in being single. These poems, quite simply, are for women who have loved.

I share them to celebrate love and loving in its full measure.

The time has come to love again, to care and dare enough to leave a poem on his pillow.

And then he came.
I wasn't looking but I was waiting.
He came with a wonderful blend of life.
And assured with a clear certainty
I wanted him to know me from the beauty of my inner being,
From haute couture to jeans,
Laughing
the gourmet of my essence,
and the spirit of my dancing
with a lovely emotional honesty.

LOVE.
Let it be and let it live.
Be on, LOVE, forever insisting.
Be on, LOVE—I insist—everlasting.

My impressions respectfully,

HOW WOULD
YOU LIKE YOUR WORLD
TODAY?

A Collection of
Contemporary Love Poetry

INVITED

I want to be invited

To love you, as you wish
Into your world
Behind the scenes of your stage
Into a new phase

I want to be invited
To your experience
To know you
Inside and out.

I don't know if
Tomorrow has a place
That we face
Together
Or if we just know
Special moments

I want to be invited
Into your space
        your life
        your bed

I await
So that I can
        R.S.V.P
Front row and center

§

ArchinG

One day when I have
a thousand years

And you're all ears
with nothing but a memory

I'm going
to extend an invitation
to explore things like
the river's bend
God's children
and the beginning of everything
never ends
it circulates.

There is no revolution
only evolutions
that never end
but just continue
throughout time
making us think
a change had occurred

I'm going to let you
hold me hostage
and show me the
bend or the arch.

The difference between
the feather and the rock
or the rock and the feather.

As you autocratically motion
these matters
I will simply contemplate
the bend of the river
your flow
and sons.

§

AN ODE TO BLACK WOMEN

The most beautiful woman in the world is your mother
because of her you become,
The famous line,
"beauty is in the eye of the beholder."
is true
Nobody knows what you see.
Who is the classic black beauty?
      she's your mother,
      she's your sister,
      she's your daughter,
      she is you.

This woman is as pretty internally as she is externally,
She may wear the latest in Paris designs
A maid's uniform may be her daily attire.
Her clothes are unimportant.
Her hair might be coiffure in the finest salons
Her beauty secrets may be well guarded in the privacy of
Her kitchen.
She may define liberation not as going to work but
By staying home being Mrs. Housewife,
She may never leave the confines of her neighborhood.
She may opt to see the world.
She may live on the limited budget of ADC
She may have a PHD.
She may protest, scrape and struggle to live
in that "better neighborhood"
She may be America's First Lady
Regal to casual
Knowing the perils of the highs and lows
Of womanhood, sisterhood and motherhood.

§

An Ode to Black Women II

She is the one Duke wrote Sophisticated Lady for.
She is the Colored Girl Who Has Considered Suicide When
the Rainbow Was Enuf.
She knows
the chicness of Chicago
the hipness of New York
the mysteries of Mississippi
the zaniness of Hollywood
the depths of Detroit
the sassiness of San Francisco
the brawniness of Birmingham
the action of Atlanta
the wickedness of Washington
the means of Memphis.
She may never visit these places
perhaps she was born there.

She may wear silk blouses unbuttoned to there
maybe she wouldn't dare.
She's easy and breezy and frightened
as she searches for herself.
She may have defined who she is and dare you to ask.

§

Photo Courtesy of ERNEST COLLINS PHOTOGRAPHY

AN ODE TO BLACK WOMEN III

She is as complex as she is simple
as sanctified as sophisticated
as old as she is young
growing everyday in a different way
Some know her, others don't recognize her name.
You know her.

> She's your mother.
> She's your sister.
> She's your aunt.
> She's your daughter.
> She's your cousin.
> She's your friend.
> She's your grandmother.
> She's your godmother.
> She's your neighbor.
> She's your niece.
> She's your baby.
> She's your lady.

§

AN ODE TO BLACK WOMEN IV

Her soul is as beautiful as her face,
as in Lena.
She may not win a beauty contest
But humbles her country's humanity,
as in Barbara.
Her country has hushed her voice
by not allowing her to sing in a Capital Hall
but the world heard and acclaimed her whispers
the nightingale of the land,
as in Marian.
She built an empire with her special ingredients
especially for Black hair
under the label of
Madam C. J.

She is famous and goes unrecognized.
She has done unique things
like taking garbage and making them greens.
Her legs have done dual things
holding her body tall and strong
testing her strength as she
scrubbed floors to raise
millionaire sons.
She may do things her mother never dreamed.
Who is she?
She's a profound woman in the midst of a profane world.

§

AN ODE TO BLACK WOMEN

She is as precious as pretty.
Ageless
as old as the Nile.
As young as the latest fad
glowing in the light of adversities.
She has preserved and protected often being neglected
She has been glue for her people.
Who is she?
She is that noble African queen
stripped of her nobility
turned nursemaid
mistress to the mighty
faithful to her family
close to her children
strong on Sunday morning
building a church.
Cool on Saturday night
curling her hair.

She's that brilliant girl standing in Little Rock
trying to go to school
She's that beauty crowned Miss Universe
both times making your heart swell,
She is the classic Black beauty
dwelling in America's soul
seen in your local community
preaching on Sunday
going to work on Monday
anticipating the fever of Saturday night.

Who is she?
She is busy in the business world
Sitting on a corporate board
a twirling tycoon
a feminist lobbying for equality
a slating stateswoman
a prophetic professor
a fashion designer
a broadway poet
a legal wizard
a delicate doctor
a majestic minister
a stunning superstar.

Who is she?
She is you.
Mother of humanity
classic in her style
black in her skin
brilliant in her beauty
ultra in her sheen.

§

A
PURPLE
MOOD

You purpled my mood
t o d a y
moving it from
a sunny sky blue
to mauve
to midnight.

When purple
I saw
my poised passion
posed in your life
remembering
your pleasure as my pulse.

Those were such perfect/precious days
when we were
possessed
with just each other.
The purpose was to play
the day gone
and to love all day long.

So, if you please
turn the purple
b a c k
to midnight
b a c k
to mauve
back
to sunny sky blue.

§

HEY OLD MAN

HEY OLD MAN

You
with the
beautiful soul
framed in snow white hair
wrapped in a wrinkled skin

You
who knows
the games people play
beforehand
and wait patiently
to learn the outcome.

You
who relates
to children
for the precious beings
they are
You
who have
toiled so long and hard
to bring us where we are
today.

Sorry,
I didn't get here sooner
so I could have
enjoyed
you longer.

§

A THOUSAND YEARS

I've known you for a thousand years
and only loved you for a day.
You've been a treasure inside of me
yet we've only embraced for a moment.
We've touched so slightly
but I feel you every day
The moments, the days, the touching, the feelings
are mere memories in my mind.
They are the most important thoughts to me.
Why did you go away?

§

A GOLD MEDAL

What is the world coming to?

A gold medal for John Wayne
What did he do?

He acted roles
at the movie show
read lines
somebody else wrote.

He was the all American male
made up
tall, big and strong
riding horses
shooting guns
rough, tough
true grit
fiction and fantasy
made him rich.

I would like to know
about the gold medal
for
another American hero

--MARTIN LUTHER KING, JR.—

Remember------------------------------
he was the one slain
for humane things

Wasn't he a good American too?

§

THE BIRTHDAY BOY COMES TO TOWN

One Christmas
a man came to town.
He heard a lot was going down.
He saw decorated trees
lights flashing
on and off of things
all of the people were as busy as bees.

He saw a jolly bearded fat man
dressed in a red velvet suit
children sat on his knee
and described things
they wanted to see
under a tree.

The man thought ----------------------------
what a strange way
to celebrate a sacred holiday.
He wanted to talk
to somebody
about the course of events.

So, the next day
he went walking down the street
and knocked on a bungalow door.

The children in the house
were laughing with glee.
The man peeked in
viewing toys, clothes and presents galore.

The lady told the gentleman
he couldn't come in
walking down the stairs.
He started to grin.
He remembered
that's what they told
his mother at the inn.

He thought after all these years
I just wanted to see
what they did to remember me
imagine going to your own birthday party
and not getting in.

On Christmas day
will you be
under the Christmas tree
to see
what Santa brought
and miss
the Messiah
knocking at the door?

§

BLUE BALLET

As I researched my life
the other night
to look at my private self
I touched a me
that I wonder if anyone knows.

There was an intellectual
pondering in innocence
the issues of the day,
the import of life
wondering who I will be
a hundred years from now
and if the rush and fuss
are really necessary.

And if I am worthy
of life
in their cruel world
wondering if my tender, delicateness
would/could
force the world
to succumb
if I were in power.

There was a soul
that aches during the day
because it's my unnatural time.
A soul that wakes
at midnight
waiting to ask questions
like,
"Jesus, why didn't you stay?"

At midnight the artist
stirs
creating things.
nobody sees
like,
dancing ballets
and understanding
the paradox of the blues
performing the blue ballet
in a sophisticated splendor
thrilled in my solitude.

Sleep comes
be patient,
the world screams
for the beginning
of a new day
is making its way
through the night.

And the sunlight
might reveal
how to let the
midnight scholar
perform the
blue ballet
in public.

§

MS. QUEEN BEE

How silly they are
asking
what should I wear
when only they care
wondering what man will appear
fearful of none
glad for anyone.

Unsatisfied with personal possessions
unknowing of worldly woes
raised to be sweet young things
ripened sour
with no place to go
but the store
for more
of the same stuff
trying to buy
emotional excitement
as an indictment
of a place in life
as somebody's wife.

Versed in language
viced in life
poor and privileged
the privileged poor
what a bore
filled with conversation
on how they sought
what they bought
with plan or purpose
but purchase after purchase
planning for paradise
with a pauper's soul.

A generation away
from burning decay
wearing gaudy Gucci
and
vulgar Vuitton
entrenched with expense
dramatic exaggerations
trying to be real
with a refined stylized phoniness.

§

BLUE BIRDS
HIGH
RISES

Cities of pavement, steel and concrete
buildings line up very neat.

Politicians, businessmen
devoting their lives to
controlling the lives of those
living in the tamed jungle.

The concrete jungle where life
has become cheap.
The newscaster told the story
where a man was killed over
a dime.

All reaching for success
and the blue bird.
Spirits and souls being
bought, sold and compromised
and at the dawning of the day
you wonder where you went.

So you stalk the concrete
jungle
searching your steel soul
stole away in a high rise.

§

CHERISHED CHILDHOOD

When I am born
again
I want it to be
in your arms.
So, you can hold me
in a way
my mother doesn't know
how.
And so,
we will have a lifetime
with a bred perspective
where we understand
moves
prior to motion
like parents know the
why
of a child's cry
before a tear appears.
Promise me a chic
Childhood
Whereby
I'm rocked to sleep
with lullabies like
Ellington's suites
Sinatra's songs
Quincy's cues
Basie's blues
Bennett's ballads
and
feed me
shrimp, lobster
gumbo and champagne
for every meal
and
at night
after you tuck me in
promise to love me
once, twice, thrice
maybe more
and keep my icy feet warm.

And as I grow up
becoming an
emotional expressionist
with poised passion
sharing sentiments of my soul
don't hold me back.
Give me direction.
Hold me
so I won't break
but give me space
to crack
and put me back
and
then when you
get to know me real well
understanding
my essence
my message
never let the child
grow/go
out of me.

§

DO
U
LOVE
ME
?

Do you love me?
You questioned.

Your eyes listening
Your fingers seeing
Watching my poise.

Your body sneaking up
Answering
What you had asked.

§

HOW WOULD
YOU LIKE YOUR WORLD
TODAY?

Can I serve it to you on gold or silver
perhaps, trimmed with lace?
How would you like to seize this place as you make your way?
What color would you make the day?

How would you have rhythm flow?
How long should the hour of the moment be?
What side of midnight would you like to see?

When would you like to be born
and who shall tender your birthrights?
What lesson of life do you find most precious?
What paradox would you have explained?
What thought makes you glisten?
Whose voice makes you listen?

Do you know time can be a lonely place
And home is a person not a place
and
that the heart turns the brain
and
rhythm is the secret to being?
Do you know what to do with the light from the moon?

Whose portrait would you paint?
Is your desire to be gracious or great
lovely, loving or love?
What secrets would expose your soul?
Where would you place the sunset
and
What do you propose for the blues?
How would you be in the world without me?
Will you remember when we made love painfully pretty?

What virtues would you give a child?
What is your noble cause?
Your private passion?
Do you follow the golden rule?
What love would you let linger?
Do you know life will make patience wait?
What moments of life would you replay?

What music makes you move?
Would you hear me if I screamed and
Would you let me listen when you shout?
What feelings would you trap in your heart?
What implosions bear repeating?

What pain could I take away?
What music could play an endless concert in your ear?
What moments make you pray?
Do you know my mind sleeps with your soul
and
when did you come best?

Why, are you so private?
When will you let me in?
What dreams will you realize?
What comforts your soul?
What will you leave the world?
What search will you find?
Will you need me when I want you
and
do you know the difference between silence,
being solitude
and
suffering in silence seeking solitude?

What art is your form?
What form will you make life?
What sense do you give this confusion?
Do you know pain doesn't hurt
if you can bear it

Do you understand?

§

HOW WOULD
YOU LIKE YOUR WORLD
TODAY?

HOW WOULD
YOU LIKE YOUR WORLD TODAY?

_____

_____

_____

_____

_____

_____

_____

_____

_____

_____

_____

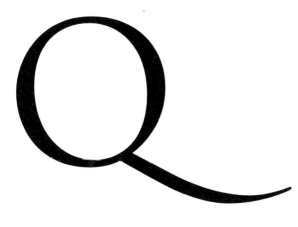

Hailing from Chicago's South Side
He made magnificent strides
From New York to L.A.
Sinatra named him Q.
The music man
With emotion lotion
Putting it in the pocket
They call him Q.

He writes,
arranges,
composes,
produces,
directs
Only for the great ones
Killer Joe to Thriller
Working with the Chairman
Brother Ray
Counting Basie's beat
Making Lady D the Queen of the scene
Feeling Heat in the Night
Making
Michael's moonwalk
To painting
 Color Purple
All in one he is from
Be Bop
To Hip Hop
How cool can you be?

His special touch
You love so much
He touches so great
Enhancing
The musical score
Making music magic

Maestro, if you please
Don't be so mean
Touch the planet
Adoring all
Being the best
Human you can be
Growing, always
Knowing what's real

All the while
Circling 360 degrees
Living, loving and learning
To the nth degree
Hip is a must
Giving the world yourself
As you move about
Without doubt
Being the creative one
In the studio, for the movies, on record
Staying ahead by ten
Then
Always knowing when the tempo is just right
Playing round bout midnight
In the jook joint
Securing your way

Yours is sincerely the best
Verbose
And beautiful
Q
The jazzman
Forever

Keep doing it
Scatting to rapping
Until you get enough
And then
Don't stop
Because
Everybody
Loves your stuff like that.

§

MAKING LOVE

You have made me come to realize
there is more to making love
than making love.

You've brought forth
the notion
as you bowed in my bones
putting me out of grace
in a delightful juxtaposition
groping for apprehension
taking emotional liberties
with me.

You've brought to my attention
the privy to my life
as I wonder what you
do with your wife.

What a disgrace to man's fortune
if he never realizes
there is more to making love
than making love.

§

NATALIE'S LIFE POEM

I'm beginning to feel life
and it's feeling just fine
I'm right on time
learning the secrets to
bend, flow and blow
life, living and loving
like
bending with rubber and steel
flowing with the river and against the sea
upstream, midstream, downstream
blowing with the wind
and breezing through the tornado

like
knowing when creativity stops it
ceases to be
if preserved
it becomes tradition
copied losing originality
then it's time to move on
to grow to dare to be different
feel what may be pain, at the time
but soon will lose it's sensation
to become a positive experience
that you one day will look back on
and laughter will grip your face
and conquests become conquered
when you cease to try.

and
how life is filled more with ironic
paradoxes, than truths
and the trick is to balance

and
a natural part of loving is pain
contradictory and contrasting
to love's literature
but literate to love's experience
like knowing
divorce is a part of marriage
and it never ever really comes
because once it begins it never ends.

like
a sophisticated lady really has class
upon touching the earthiness
in her bones
when she defines and defies
times, places, postures and positions
seeking her own single savage solitude
bearing no explanation
except a primitive
"I want to"
It's the essence of Cole Porter's
"The Lady Is a Tramp"
The art is being a stable butterfly
reaching, perching and only
getting caught when you want to.

Like
knowing the perfect lover
is not the one who moves
your perfect body
but the one
who holds hands with your soul
touching the raw nerve
the guts of marrow
invisible
until touched
that's the one you will love forever
feeling he is the reason you were born,

Like
recognizing the difference
between
falling in love
loving
and being loved
In each instance being lovely.

Be a woman of substance
aloof in your approach
caring, touching and feeling
as you soar
hearing, listening and making
life's music
and remember
don't wait too long
to love.

§

FOR
CONFUSED
COUPLES

I know where you are
we've been there too
I saw his hurt, anger, dismay and pain
as he tried to figure out what to do.

He traveled your road
wore your shoes
looked your look.

He said, the light in the universe
seemed out
I said, they're not
a long blink
but the sun and stars
are bound to shine
he said, the brightness of color
seemed bleached out
I said,
let's buy Tide
He said, the melody of the song
seemed gone
I said,
listen to the birds outside.

I tried to
put glitter into his gloom
passion into his pain
purpose into his blues
love into his loneliness
romance into his reality

And one day
we woke up
and it was gone.

§

IF I COULD CONSTRUCT
YOU A DAY

I'd make it night
And the breeze would stir to sounds
of Nancy and Dinah in your ear
And whenever you wanted a majestic moment,
hilltops, a glistening lake and sunrises
would appear.

Words would flow from your mind
through your pen
And other words would be written for you alone
to compliment your moods and sentiments
And I would send you around the world in a day
So, you wouldn't be gone away too long.

And when you wanted the hecticness of the day to stop
It would suddenly be still.

And be
as revealing as the water gently striking the shores
And after your brief encounter with your
private self
The day would continue.

And somewhere along the way
You'd stop to smell a flower
and watch the children at play
Which is really God's way
of saying, "Hey".

And as you soothed your soul
by sipping your cognac you would take love,
feel the feelings
that make for endurance
when all else is doubtful.

And when the eloquence of evening approached
your introspections and reflections
would make for a mellow mood
And right before the silence of your slumber
you would articulate and communicate
in the language only lovers know.

And only then
after you have tired of life's bouquet
long after the anxieties and problems of the day
have been loved away
you would sleep long and when you stirred
caresses would greet you
And we'd wait for
the dawning of a brand new day.

§

HAVE YOU EVER MADE LOVE TO A DANCER?

The older man
asked the younger
"Have you ever made love to a dancer?"

The older man told why he should
He said,
she would
dance as they lay,
her arms rendering him motionless.

He said,
she would direct his moments of moves
striking the right rhythm
and he wouldn't know
slow from fast
but would graciously groove.

He said,
the dancer's moves are inbred
when she flows into you
you float
and when she
sways a bit
you will think
this is it
and glide
right across the room.

He said,
her body would respond
with hellos
and she would
turn and turn and turn
to a marvelous beat.

He said,
on the final turn
you will yearn
then she will twirl
you will swirl
then she will leap
you will jump
then she will pause
you will wait
for the next step.

The younger man
asked,
did it matter whether she
did a ballet or the boogie?

The elder replied,
the dancer
will take you from the ballet to the boogie
and when she's balleting you will boogie
and when she's boogieing you will ballet
and when she's done
you will have discoed
and
you won't know the ballet from the boogie.

He said,
her love will always linger
in your life
and you shall always smile
and that's why
you should lay with a dancer.

I thought their conversation interesting,
decided
to leave the men
to their talk
and
I just danced
myself right out the room.

§

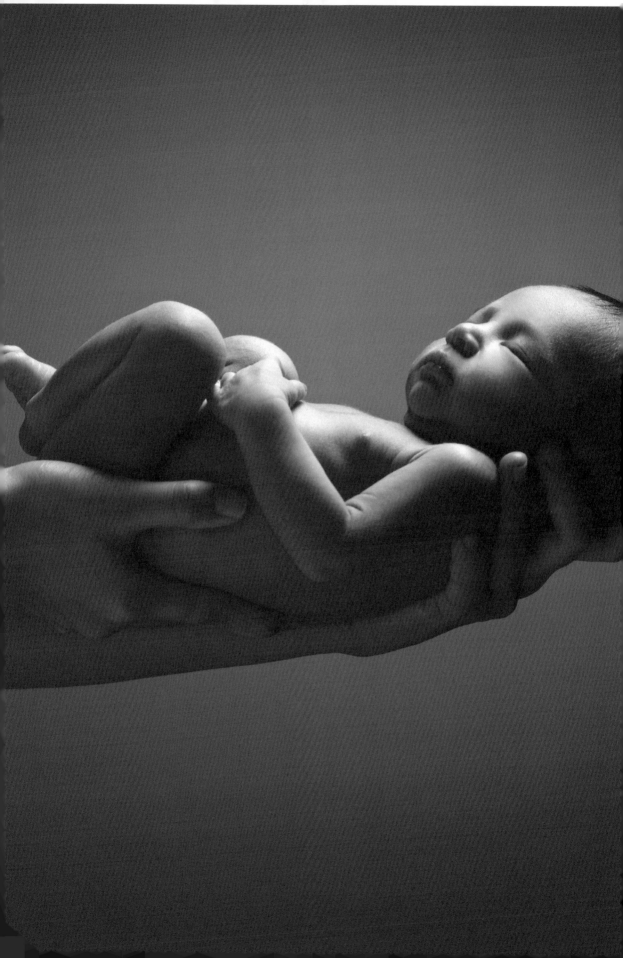

NOW I LAY ME DOWN

Now I lay me
down to thee
what shall we be?

The emotional position
is beyond love
it's a united trilogy
it's life touching
its amazing self
asking for nothing
wanting everything

§

ON THE DAY

One day when you're old
and the world has exposed itself to you

On the day when you wink
at the sun saying,
I know why you shine

On the day you remember
your renaissance
and reveal your rendezvous with you

On the day you correct your erroneous zones
and reckon life is not age but stages and cycles

On the day you peak in your personhood
and realize you did all you could

On the day you peek at the moon
remembering whispers and weaknesses
and understand the existence of midnight

On the day you grip
the passages of passion

On the day you touch
the stillness of silence
to calm the stirring of the soul

On the day you realize
the life you subscribe
to is good
and the one others describe
is good too
but not for you

On the day you learn
the external world is
controlled by the internal self
and little else matters

On those days
when things come about
I hope you will remember
wearing me
with a lovely love
so profound
it is defined
making me, making you
making us
HAPPY

§

ON THE DAY DUKE DIED

On the day Duke died
I cried
Not knowing why.

The radio played his music all day long
sweet, sensuous, sensitive sounds
soothed my soul.
I thought of delicate, debonair dashing ------------------------
Duke
as my very own

The man who called music his mistress
a poet of life
a master of mystery.
how fortunate
your lover
I thought,
as I read your book
cringed with jealousy.
How lucky
is she
to have known you.

How fortunate are we
that you shared your love affair with the world.
And to get involved
all one had to do
was listen
as we conducted our
own
love affairs.

How lonely your mistress
must be
How grateful is she
for you
wore her well.

The day Duke died
I cried
now I know why
because
I'm the Sophisticated Lady
who took the "A" Train
to the
Lush Life

§

TIME
TABLE

Birthdays are God's appointments
for arrival
It is his own personal statement
on your time, space and place
in His universe.

Life is your message to God
as to how worthy you are of
occupying space in his place
Life is time between appointments.

Death is God's appointment
for departure
to another
time, space and place.

§

POISED PASSION

There is a soul
akin to me
that you know so well
stirring for release.

A mood
purpled with passion
leaping------------------uncontrollably
seeking to communicate
with encounters beyond self.

A mood
that says
if you hold me
it will set me free.

§

SUNDAY MORNING THOUGHTS

I want you to know the woman in me
Therefore.
I'm unsure if you need to see
rollers in my hair
or awake to the mess of me
or discuss the bills to be paid
or hear the worry of work

I want you to know
champagne and cognac
with a scent of sweet flowers
that are hand-picked
to sounds of Bill, Bennett, Nina
complemented with midnight apple pie

The romance in me is what
I want you to know, love
and never let go,
letting you lose yourself
Find me in a wonderfully, fresh,
exciting way
and let me love me, only to discover you
with no sense of control
always asking, how did it all happen,
is this really the result of a new kitchen?

How we always sleep tenderly
and never dare
without making love, in some lovely way
while seeking solitude in slumber in your arms
with me letting you know
I've never been a woman
with a man
wondering if you are better with me
as your woman, or the wife, in your life
desirous to be your very dearest friend.

May midnight to dawn
be forever our special time
to casually sleep
and hold secret conversations
listening and exposing
the soul of ourselves
speaking of the past only to meet the future
trying to figure ballet into baseball
Don't really know
if I want you to see
rollers in my hair
to change your
perspective
that might lead to another

How do I love you totally
without becoming mundanely
married.

§

THE QUEST TO BE

As we wander this world
in search of our selves
in securing our souls
One simply seeks to be.

As we look for ourselves in others
and we proclaim others existing and stirring in our being
As we seek our own space and place
discovering your space may rest nowhere
but your spirit may be found everywhere
One's search
is the quest to be.

As we hide from the pain of life, love and living
and rush to the passions of the same
As we grow into the art of living
learning the direction and purpose of our being
As we learn the postures to assume
turning negatives into positives
one merely quests to be.

In the end ----- when it is all said and done
after the rules of the role have been established
marks have been made.
profanities become profound
the lessons of life have been learned
loves and lovers have been shared,
come and gone

One decides
there is nothing to life
but the
quest to be.

§

VALENTINE

As I stop to reflect, to inspect the inwards
of the making of us
I feel a beautiful you.

A smile strikes my face
impressed with your glow
touching/hearing you

laugh and love
love and laugh

A perfection making
pain ignorant
beauty arrogant
life saying
live to the brink
perched on the cutting edge
dwell in the depth
hold hands with my soul
as we bathe.

I want you to have a gift
named ME
knowing
If I could make me a man
it would be
you.

I ponder all this
as I wonder
how I will pay for you.

§

FOR
MIKKI

May the magic/majesty/masterful moments
of life
freeze for you
and the days
be as gorgeous as a pretty picture

and the nights
be filled with the good things of the day
that spill over into the night
because the day is not long enough
to enjoy

and may the days ahead
be filled with splendid sunrises
and bright horizons

that make for a
pretty life.

§

RESPONDING

I had to go
      To leave the world for a moment
I tired you so
      You were my strength
      You understood my struggle
         My strife, even my life better than me.

I'm glad you were there
      You wore me well.
Now you must rest
      As I overcome this hell
Alone.

Your tenderness has touched me
      In a way unknown
Giving me what I needed
      Before I desired it
      Just as I was preparing for it

As I search for myself
      I am constantly finding you
I hope to grow up one day - mature as they say
But I'll never stop reaching for you
      Dear precious one.

§

BE YOURSELF

Be yourself
know yourself
there is no genie in the bottle for you.

You are too unique.
too beautiful

It is not in the clothes that you wear
it is the style

It is not the furniture
it is the home

It is not the copy of friend
it is the friendship

It is not the common of the wares
it is the beauty of you

It is not the gift you buy
it is not the expense
It is the thought
because
the gift is really you.

It is time and commitment
not jealousy and fame
it is wonders never cease
friendship grows and becomes
more endured
it is the fellowship
it is the feeling

It is the reach
of love
It is finding your very own
rainbow

Be Yourself

§

I SEE YOUR FACE ON MY PILLOW

I see your face on my pillow
Radiant and
Smiling with a wise love
Hoping for the unknown
Looking with mystery
looming and blooming
To sooth past hurts
With future possibilities.

Scared to
But scared not to
I see your face on my pillow
Waiting to unfold
With motions and notions
With love to come
Waiting for arms to hold just you
And watch you stir

I see your face on my pillow
Waiting for the best to come
To you and for you
From me
Making us.

§

MAKE YOUR MUSIC

I want to hear your music
I want to hear you sing
I want to see you smile
I want to write you a song
    With lyrics
That make you play the piano
Appreciating your talent
That makes you smile
With your eyes.

I want to make you realize you
As I realize me
As we make each other be

I want to hear your music
I want to hear you sing
Your very own song.

§

PAULA'S POEM

When you're a little girl
growing up
you have no idea who you're
being influenced by.

You simply know you're
having fun
playing with your little cousins
running in the snow
skipping in the sun.

How happy am I today
in my grown stage of youth
to have had you in my formative years
molding me into what
I have become.

I thank you for being,
sharing yourself with me
in a way
words will never explain
and only feelings of love
can approach in explanation.

With much love
may today
be the happiest in your life
as I have grown
to learn the woes of womanhood
and loves of life.
I rejoice in your birth
-----Paula Jean-----
and I am glad
there is you
and you have participated
in the making of me.

§

FOR PAMELA

What do people do while waiting
for something to happen?

What do people do while waiting
for the results to come in?

What do people do while sitting on the sidelines
watching the mainline
realizing this is what I have been waiting for?

We are the ones we are waiting for.
What do people do while waiting
the free ones, the independent ones, the declared ones
the undecided ones?

What do people do while waiting?
They decide what to do.

Waiting for the leader to step up
to divide their souls
to play their music
to move into action

People wait and groove
while waiting for the next best thing
so they can join in.

§

HEY JESUS

HEY JESUS,
why didn't you stay?
what made you go away?
Did you really go for me?
Do you hear me when I pray?

Dear Jesus, why did you go away?
HEY JESUS,
was it hard being a Jew
    or
was it harder being you?

HEY JESUS,
why didn't you stay
to help with life's lessons?
Did you leave us the answers?
Are they really written in a book?

HEY JESUS,
did you bite off more than
you could chew?

HEY JESUS,
why did they kill you?
for doing what you do?
Did you commit suicide?
Did you really die?

HEY JESUS,
why did you come this way?
If I invite you back
will you stay?

If you come back today
what would you say
about the current human condition
    and
what is man's real state of affairs
     and
how do you feel about
the fight over your land
and Egypt's revolution?

HEY JESUS,
would you marry Mary
this time
and
how would you look
on TV?
Could you explain sexuality
and
what makes the sun rise and set
differently?

HEY JESUS,
WHY DIDN'T YOU STAY?

§

die liebe

amour

SZERETET

IRMASTUS

애정

kaerlighed

kärlek

喜爱

SAYANG

láska

LOVE

amore

For Booking and/or Purchase
contact

HARTMAN PUBLISHING GROUP
19 North Sangamon
Chicago, Illinois 60607-2613
312/822..0202
www.ndigo.com

Visit HERMENE HARTMAN
at

FaceBook

HOW WOULD YOU LIKE YOUR WORLD TODAY?

CPSIA information can be obtained
at www.ICGtesting.com

226152LV00001BC